Contents

Some words are printed in bold, **like this**. You can find out what they mean on page 30. You can also look in the box at the bottom of the page where they first appear.

Every contact leaves a trace

There has been a robbery. The thief is gone. There were no witnesses. There is no video. How can the police find the thief? It is time to call in the **forensic investigators**. Forensic investigators use science to solve crimes.

Scientists want to find the answer to a question. So, they make a prediction. A prediction is a good guess. Then they find **evidence**. Evidence is information they can use to test their prediction. Scientists make **observations**. They take measurements. Taking careful notes and keeping good records are very important.

Forensic investigators also find evidence. They test it at crime labs. The evidence helps them find out who did the crime.

Forensic investigators will look for clues that the thief left behind.

evidence information or objects that can help prove a prediction
forensic used for the law
investigator person who tries to find the answer to a question
observation careful look at something

Forensic Investigator

Susan Glass

www.raintreepublishers.co.uk

Visit our website to find out more information about **Raintree** books.

To order:

☎ Phone 44 (0) 1865 888112

🖹 Send a fax to 44 (0) 1865 314091

💻 Visit the Raintree Bookshop at **www.raintreepublishers.co.uk** to browse our catalogue and order online.

First published in Great Britain by Raintree,
Halley Court, Jordan Hill, Oxford OX2 8EJ,
part of Harcourt Education.
Raintree is a registered trademark of Harcourt
Education Ltd.

© Harcourt Education Ltd 2008
First published in paperback in 2008
The moral right of the proprietor has been asserted.

Editorial: Nancy Dickmann and Claire Throp
Design: Philippa Jenkins and Q2A Creative
Illustrations: Mark Preston
Picture Research: Mica Brancic
Production: Alison Parsons

Originated by Modern Age
Printed and bound in China by Leo Paper Group

ISBN 978 1 4062 0733 0 (hardback)
12 11 10 09 08
10 9 8 7 6 5 4 3 2 1

ISBN 978 1 4062 0747 7 (paperback)
12 11 10 09 08
10 9 8 7 6 5 4 3 2 1

**British Library Cataloguing in Publication
Data**
Glass, Susan
Forensic Investigator. – (Fusion)
363.2'5
A full catalogue record for this book is available from
the British Library.

Acknowledgements
The publishers would like to thank the following
for permission to reproduce photographs: Alamy/
Ian Miles-Flashpoint Pictures pp. **12**, **13**; Alamy p.
15 (Mikael Karlsson); Alamy/vario images GmbH
& Co.KG p. **25** (Ulrich Baumgarten); Corbis pp.
11 (Silvia Morara), **16** (Andrew Brookes), **28** (Ralf-
Finn Hestoft), **17**; Corbis/ZUMA p. **26** (Ruaridh
Stewart); Getty Images/PhotoDisc p. **14**; Photolibrary.
com/Blend Images Llc p. **20** (Jose Luis Pelaez Inc);
Photolibrary.com/Index Stock Imagery p. **9** (Gary
Conner); Popperfoto p. **23**; Rex Features p. **5**
(Anthony Hammond); Science Photo Library p. **19**
(Mauro Fermariello); Science Photo Library/Peter
Arnold Inc. p. **7** (Volker Steger).

Cover photograph of a silhouette of a man against
fingerprint background reproduced with permission
of Getty Images (Photographer's Choice/David
McGlynn).

Every effort has been made to contact copyright
holders of any material reproduced in this book. Any
omissions will be rectified in subsequent printings if
notice is given to the publishers.

The publishers would like to thank Nancy Harris and
Harold Pratt for their assistance with the preparation
of this book.

Disclaimer
All the Internet addresses (URLs) given in this book
were valid at the time of going to press. However,
due to the dynamic nature of the Internet, some
addresses may have changed, or sites may have
changed or ceased to exist since publication. While
the author and publishers regret any inconvenience
this may cause readers, no responsibility for any
such changes can be accepted by either the author
or the publishers.

It is recommended that adults supervise children on
the Internet.

Casebook

The thief left evidence at the crime scene. The scene left evidence on him, too. Forensic investigators will find this evidence. You can follow their investigation in this casebook.

Making predictions

Forensic investigators are scientists. They ask a question. Then, they predict (guess) what the answer will be. This prediction is called a **hypothesis**. In this case the question is, "Who is the thief?" One hypothesis could be that a certain **suspect** (person) did it. Now the hypothesis must be proved.

The forensic team look for **evidence** to prove the hypothesis. For example, they might look for hair or mud. They send it to the crime lab. Scientists there test it. Their careful notes and measurements are also evidence.

Forensic investigators may measure a footprint. They measure it to see if it matches a suspect's shoe. Sometimes they measure how far apart footprints are. This helps them **estimate** (guess) a person's height. They make sure their measurements are right. If they are wrong, the police might arrest the wrong suspect.

Even tiny pieces of evidence are useful. This investigator is looking for fingerprints.

estimate   use evidence to guess how much something is
hypothesis   possible answer to a question
suspect   person the police think might have committed a crime

First things first

After a crime the police are called. First, they tape off the crime scene. They make sure no one touches anything. That would make it harder to get **accurate** (correct) measurements.

Next, the police call the **forensic** team. The forensic team are scientists who look for **evidence** to help solve the crime. The forensic **investigators** take photos. They make sketches of the scene. They carefully measure the room. Their sketches will show the size of the room in metres and centimetres. The drawing helps people at the lab picture the crime scene.

In this case the thief broke a window to get in. This is a good place to look for footprints and fingerprints. The team looks around the window. They carefully record everything they find.

accurate exactly right, correct

Forensic investigators bring a number of tools to the crime scene.

CRIME SCENE DO NOT CROSS

True crime

Investigators once found a thief's wallet by a broken window. It fell out when he squeezed through. A card in the wallet gave them his name and address!

Fingerprints

Fingerprints are good **evidence**. They can be used to identify the person who left them. That is because no two people have the same prints. Everyone's fingerprints are different.

The team uses magnifying glasses to help find prints. Magnifying glasses make things look larger. This makes things easier to see. The prints get brushed with powder. Then, they are lifted with tape. The team takes photos of the prints.

Police keep a file of fingerprints. Computers can tell if a fingerprint matches one from the file. They do this by comparing different parts of the print. They compare the shape and size of the print.

whorl

arch

loop

There are three main shapes of fingerprint: whorls, arches, and loops. Which type do you have? You may have a mix.

brush fingerprints with a special powder. It makes them easier to see.

Casebook

Fingerprints were found and sent to the lab. The computer found two matches. One print matches **suspect** (person) A. The other matches suspect B. Both worked here months ago as furniture movers. Did one come back to steal?

Footprints

The team finds a footprint in the mud. It is by the broken window. They measure it carefully. This is so they can find out the shoe size. They can even work out what type of shoe made the print.

The team takes photos of the print. They place a measurement scale next to the footprint. The scale looks like a ruler. It shows the size of the footprint.

A ruler is put next to the footprint. It shows how big the footprint is.

cast copy of a shape, made by pouring a liquid into

Investigators also make a **cast** (hard copy) of the footprint. They mix powder with water. They pour it into the print. It hardens to make a cast. The cast shows more detail than a photo.

Investigators mix water with white powder to make a cast of the footprint.

Casebook

A footprint cast is taken. It is the right size for both **suspects**. There are no shoe matches yet.

Tools and tool marks

The thief tried to force the window open. The tool he used left a mark in the wood. **Investigators** measure the mark. They make a **cast** (hard copy). They send it to the lab.

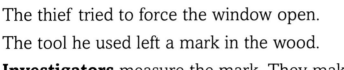

> Tools can be matched to marks they leave at the scene.

Casebook

The thief tried to open the window with a tool. It was probably a crowbar. The forensic team makes a cast of the mark. Now they must try to find the tool that made it.

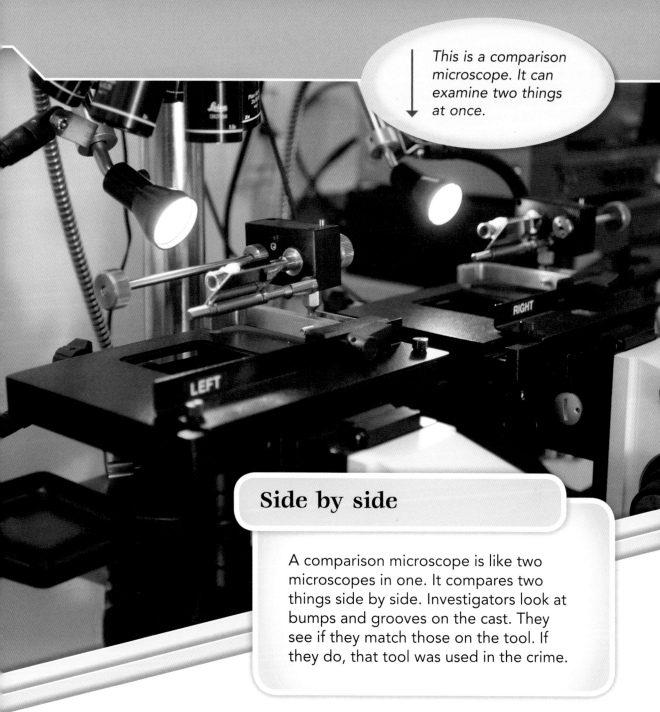

This is a comparison microscope. It can examine two things at once.

LEFT

RIGHT

Side by side

A comparison microscope is like two microscopes in one. It compares two things side by side. Investigators look at bumps and grooves on the cast. They see if they match those on the tool. If they do, that tool was used in the crime.

Microscopes are important tools in crime labs. Many pieces of **evidence** are too small to see clearly. Microscopes help the investigators to see them better. **Forensic** investigators use many types of microscope. To examine the tool marks, they use a comparison microscope.

15

DNA

The team finds an important clue. It is on the broken window. The thief cut himself on the glass when he climbed through. There is blood on the glass. The **investigators** take a sample of the blood.

Casebook

Blood from the crime scene is sent to the lab for DNA testing (see box on page 17). DNA samples are taken from both suspects. One of them may be a match.

DNA can be found in blood, hair, or saliva (spit).

database large amount of information stored in a computer

DNA something that is found in all living things

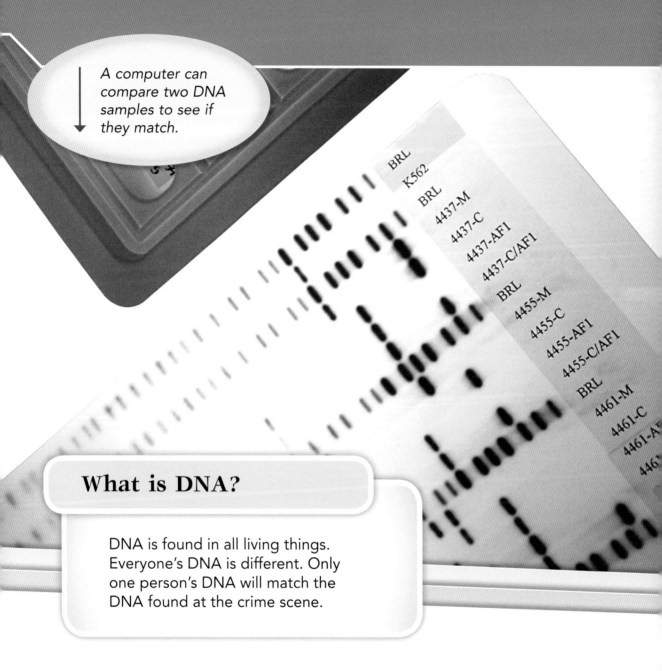

A computer can compare two DNA samples to see if they match.

BRL
K562
BRL
4437-M
4437-C
4437-AF1
4437-C/AF1
BRL
4455-M
4455-C
4455-AF1
4455-C/AF1
BRL
4461-M
4461-C
4461-A
446

What is DNA?

DNA is found in all living things. Everyone's DNA is different. Only one person's DNA will match the DNA found at the crime scene.

Blood can be an important piece of **evidence**. Blood contains **DNA** (see box). Scientists in the lab keep the DNA. They may be able to match it to a person. They might use a computer **database**. The database lists all the other DNA kept in the lab. This helps them to match the DNA to a sample taken from a **suspect** (person).

Trace evidence

The team must search the crime scene very carefully. Even tiny things, like dirt, can be **evidence**. Very small pieces of evidence are called **trace evidence**. Tiny **fibres** (threads) from clothes can be trace evidence. So can paint from a car. Even hair can be trace evidence.

Investigators try to match evidence from the crime scene to traces found on a **suspect** (person). If they find a match, it proves that the suspect was there. The team uses a **microscope** to find matches.

When a window breaks, pieces of glass fly around. Some fly towards the person breaking in. Tiny pieces end up on the person's clothes. The team will look at the glass from the crime scene. They will try to match it with one of the suspects.

Casebook

Police search both suspects' homes. They take shoes and crowbars. They take clothes to check for glass. They send everything to the crime lab.

Tiny fibres may look the same. You need a microscope to see the difference.

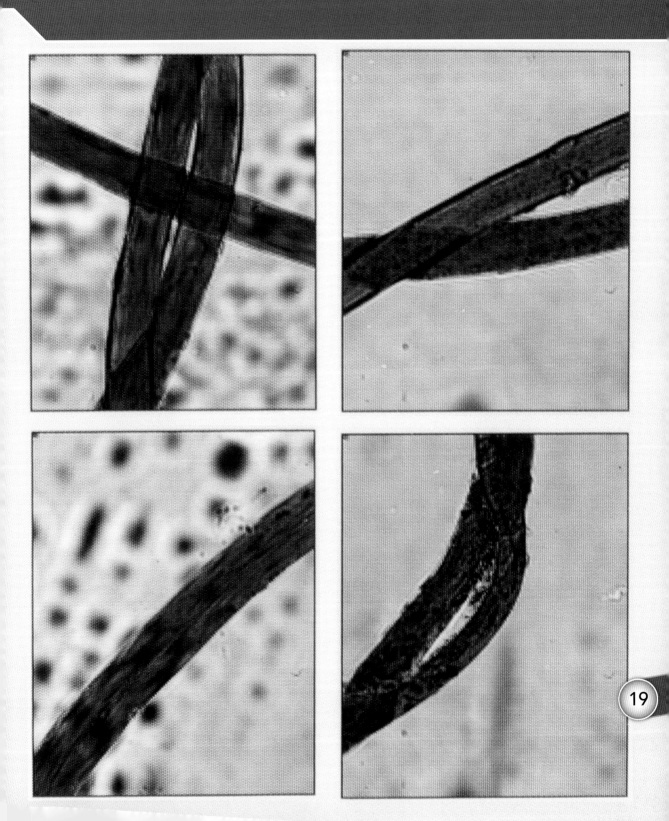

Glass

Does glass from the clothes match the window? There are several different ways to test this. The team could measure the **density** of the glass. Density is how heavy an object is for its size.

To find an object's density, the team must measure its **mass**. The mass of an object is the amount of material in it. Mass is measured in milligrams, grams, or kilograms. The team uses scales to measure mass.

Graduated cylinders are used to measure the volume of liquids.

density how heavy an object is for its size
graduated cylinder container for measuring liquids
mass amount of matter in something
volume amount of space something takes up

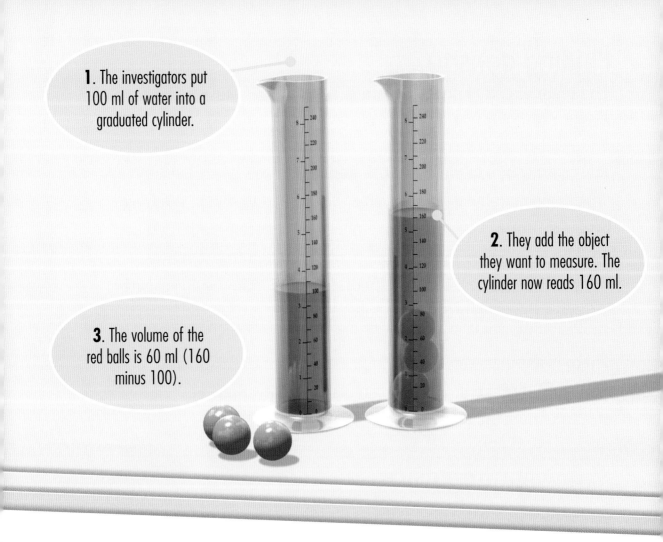

1. The investigators put 100 ml of water into a graduated cylinder.

2. They add the object they want to measure. The cylinder now reads 160 ml.

3. The volume of the red balls is 60 ml (160 minus 100).

Investigators then find the object's **volume**. Volume is the amount of space something takes up. They pour water into a measuring container. The container is called a **graduated cylinder**. A graduated cylinder measures volume. It has millilitres and litres marked on its side.

The investigators pour water into the cylinder. They read the side of the cylinder. They write down how many millilitres of water are in the cylinder. Next, they add the piece of glass. The water level rises. The volume of the glass can now be measured. The side of the cylinder is read again.

Finding density

The team already knows the **mass** of the glass. Mass is the amount of material in something.

The team wants to work out the **density** of the glass. Density is how heavy an object is for its size. They need to divide the mass by the **volume**. Volume is the amount of space something takes up. The team know the volume. Now they need to use maths. They will then know the density of the glass. They will measure the glass from the broken window.

There is another way to match glass. You can check how light goes through it. The lab can also see if two pieces of glass crack the same way.

Ancient forensics

A man called Archimedes lived more than 2,000 years ago. His king wanted to find out if a crown was pure gold. First, Archimedes used water to find the crown's volume. Next, he weighed the crown. He weighed the same volume of pure gold. The pure gold was heavier. This proved the crown was not all gold. Cheaper metal was mixed in. The crown maker had cheated the king!

Archimedes was an important scientist. He helped work out how to measure volume.

At the crime lab

A crime lab is a type of science lab. Scientists and **forensic investigators** use many of the same tools. For example, they use high-tech tools such as **microscopes**. They use them to look at tiny pieces of **evidence**.

After the robbery, evidence was taken. It was sent to the crime lab. The team **analysed** (studied) the evidence. They matched it to samples from the **suspects**. Careful measurement is important. The evidence may be used in court against a suspect. The lab team must make sure it is correct.

The lab team matched the shoe-print **cast** (hard copy) to one suspect's shoe. They measured the glass from his shirt. It matched the window. They matched his crowbar to the marks on the window. His **DNA** matched the blood from the crime scene.

Casebook

The investigators took evidence from suspect B. They took clothes and a crowbar from him. They took a shoe and DNA from him. This evidence matches the evidence from the crime scene. He is the thief!

Arrested!

Every criminal leaves something behind at the crime
scene. Every criminal also carries something away.
It could be dirt or hair. It could be a piece of glass.
It could be a **fibre** (thread) from a carpet.

Casebook

The evidence proves **suspect** B was the thief. The police show him all the proof. He admits he did it. He is arrested and must give back the stolen goods.

CASE CLOSED

Forensic investigators search the crime scene carefully. They find **evidence**. They send it to the crime lab. The team there tests and studies it. They must make sure their measurements are correct. If not, the police may arrest the wrong person.

Forensic investigators can make life harder for criminals. But they make life safer for the rest of us!

Metric matters

There are two ways of measuring things (see page 29). One is called imperial. Imperial measurements use inches and pounds. The other way is called metric. The metric system uses metres and grams. Most crime labs use metric measurements.

The suspect has been caught. Another crime has been solved by forensic science!

Amazing forensics

Forensic science is amazing. Here are some forensic facts you may not have known:

One hair can be enough to prove guilt. In one case, it was hair from a cat!

Forensic **investigators** can match a **suspect's** teeth. They match them with a bite mark on someone else.

Some people have been set free by new **DNA** testing on old **evidence**. DNA is found in all living things. It was not used when they were found guilty.

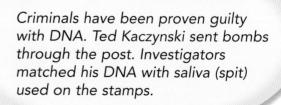

Criminals have been proven guilty with DNA. Ted Kaczynski sent bombs through the post. Investigators matched his DNA with saliva (spit) used on the stamps.

In the United Kingdom, police and labs use both metric measurements and imperial measurements.

METRIC

Length
1 metre = 100 centimetres (cm)
1 metre = 1,000 millimetres (mm)
1,000 metres = 1 kilometre (km)

Volume
1 litre (l) = 1,000 millilitres (ml)
1 cubic centimetre (cu cm) = 1 millilitre

Mass
1,000 milligram (mg) =1 gram (g)
1,000 grams = 1 kilogram (kg)

IMPERIAL

Length
1 foot (ft) = 12 inches (in)
1 yard (yd) = 3 feet
1 mile (mi) = 5,280 feet

Volume
1 cup = 8 liquid ounces (oz)
1 pint (pt) = 2 cups
1 quart (qt) = 2 pints
1 gallon (gal) = 4 quarts

Mass
1 pound (lb) = 16 ounces (oz)
1 ton = 2,000 pounds

Glossary

accurate exactly right, correct. Forensic measurement must be accurate.

analyse divide something into parts to study it. Investigators analyse clues left at a crime scene.

cast copy of a shape, made by pouring a liquid into the shape, which then hardens. Investigators make casts of tyre tracks and footprints.

database large amount of information stored in a computer. Police can search a database to find a match for a fingerprint.

density how heavy an object is for its size. Density is found by dividing an object's mass by its volume.

DNA something that is found in all living things. Each person's DNA is different from everyone else's.

estimate use evidence to guess how much something is. Scientists estimate when they cannot take exact measurements.

evidence information or objects that can help prove a prediction. Evidence is often used in court.

fibre thread, or thread-shaped part. A carpet fibre can prove that someone was at a crime scene.

forensic used for the law. Forensic science helps solve crimes.

graduated cylinder container for measuring liquids. A graduated cylinder can measure very small amounts.

hypothesis possible answer to a question. Testing and evidence prove a hypothesis right or wrong.

investigator person who tries to find the answer to a question. Forensic investigators try to find out who committed a crime.

mass amount of matter in something. Mass can be measured with scales.

microscope tool that makes tiny things appear larger. Forensic scientists look at fibres under a microscope.

observation careful look at something.

suspect person the police think might have committed a crime. Forensic investigators try to link a suspect to a crime scene.

trace evidence tiny piece of evidence. Hair, dirt, and fibres are all trace evidence.

volume amount of space something takes up. Volume can be measured in litres, millilitres, or cubic centimetres.

Want to know more?

Books to read

- *Fingerprint Evidence*, Barbara B. Rollins and Michael Dahl (Capstone Press, 2004)

- *How to Be a Scientist: Prove It!: Scientific Enquiry in Action*, Susan Glass (Heinemann Library, 2006)

- *True Crime: Crime Scenes*, John Townsend (Raintree, 2005)

Website

- http://www.unc.edu/~rowlett/units/
  Take a look at this site to find out more about imperial and metric measurements.

Read more about analysing data in *Safari Adventure*.

Find out how doctors use science to stop disease in *Has a Cow Saved Your Life?*

Index